ANIMAL KINGDOM
INSECTS

Written by
Rebecca Phillips-Bartlett

Genius Kid

American adaptation copyright © 2026 by North Star Editions, Mendota Heights, MN 55120. All rights reserved. No part of this book may be reproduced or utilized in any form or by any means without written permission from the publisher.

Insects © 2024 BookLife Publishing
This edition is published by arrangement with BookLife Publishing

sales@northstareditions.com | 888-417-0195

Library of Congress Control Number:
2024952954

ISBN
978-1-952455-31-5 (library bound)
978-1-952455-87-2 (paperback)
978-1-952455-68-1 (epub)
978-1-952455-51-3 (hosted ebook)

Printed in the United States of America
Mankato, MN
092025

Written by:
Rebecca Phillips-Bartlett

Edited by:
Elise Carraway

Designed by:
Ker Ker Lee

All facts, statistics, web addresses and URLs in this book were verified as valid and accurate at time of writing. No responsibility for any changes to external websites or references can be accepted by either the author or publisher.

Photo Credits – Images are courtesy of Shutterstock.com. With thanks to Getty Images, Thinkstock Photo and iStockphoto.

Cover – irin-k, Darkdiamond67, Butterfly Hunter, Kovalchuk Oleksandr, Protasov AN, Africa Studio, iDef Images, Kwangmoozaa. 2–3 – Eric Isselee, AlDAsign. 4–5 – dwi putra stock, Vitalii Hulai, Butterfly Hunter, Eric Isselee, Vova Shevchuk. 6–7 – alslutsky. 8–9 – Eric Isselee, Super Prin, skynetphoto, Darkdiamond67, irin-k. 10–11 – apiguide, Vitolga, moskvich1977. 12–13 – Artush, Guillermo Guerao Serra, frank60, Manfred Ruckszio. 14–15 – Tsekhmister, Henrik Larsson, Narupon Nimpaiboon. 16–17 – Breck P. Kent, mynewturtle, Leena Robinson, Butterfly Hunter. 18–19 – Vinicius R. Souza, Bill Roque, Chanachola, guy42. 20–21 – HHelene, Mongkolchon Akesin, Ama la Vida TV from Ecuador, CC BY-SA 2.0 <https://creativecommons.org/licenses/by-sa/2.0>, via Wikimedia Commons, M.Aurelius, nechaevkon. 22–23 – everydayplus, kckate16, supasart meekumrai, EcoPrint, Eric Isselee, Andrew Buckin, Chase D'animulls.

CONTENTS

Page 4   Insects
Page 6   Body of an Insect
Page 8   Types of Insects
Page 10   Habitats
Page 12   Amazing Insect Abilities
Page 14   Helpful Insects
Page 16   Life Cycle of a Butterfly
Page 18   Life Cycle of a Grasshopper
Page 20   Believe It or Not!
Page 22   Are You a Genius Kid?
Page 24   Glossary and Index

Words that look like this can be found in the glossary on page 24.

INSECTS

Most of the animal species on Earth are insects. Do you know any insects? What do they look like?

Insects are small animals with exoskeletons. An exoskeleton is a hard covering that supports and protects some animals' bodies.

DID YOU KNOW?
Hard exoskeletons mean insects do not need bones.

All insects have six legs. They have antennae on their heads. Most insects have two pairs of wings. Some have no wings at all.

DID YOU KNOW?
Spiders are not insects. Can you figure out why?

BODY OF AN INSECT

All adult insects have three main body parts.

Antennae

Mandibles

HEAD
The head is home to the insect's eyes, mouthparts, and antennae. Insects use their antennae to taste, smell, and feel. Some insects have mandibles.

THORAX

The thorax is the middle part of an insect's body. The legs and wings are attached to this part of the body.

Wings

ABDOMEN

The abdomen is the largest part of an insect's body. Most insects breathe through tiny holes on the sides of their abdomens and thoraxes.

TYPES OF INSECTS

There are over one million types of insects. Here are some you might recognize:

Ants live in groups called colonies. Each colony is led by a queen.

Queen ant

Dragonflies can fly in any direction—even backwards! Their huge eyes help them see almost all the way around themselves.

Butterflies come in many different colors. Many have patterned wings to <u>camouflage</u> themselves.

Honey bees <u>communicate</u> using something called a waggle dance.

DID YOU KNOW?
The sound of a bee buzzing is actually the sound of its wings flapping!

HABITATS

A habitat is a plant or animal's natural home. A habitat has everything a plant or animal needs to live. Habitats include food, water, and shelter.

Whirligig beetles live on water.

Many lanternflies live in <u>tropical</u> rainforests.

Many insects live under logs, among leaves, or in the ground. These are microhabitats. A microhabitat is a small area that is different than the surrounding area.

This forest is warm and dry, but these rotting logs are cool and damp.

11

AMAZING INSECT ABILITIES

Insects have <u>adaptations</u> to help them live in their environments.

MASTERS OF CAMOUFLAGE

Many insects are good at camouflaging. Some stick insects even camouflage their eggs to look like seeds.

A POWERFUL DEFENSE

Some insects pack a powerful sting. If they are in danger, they fight back. They sting their attacker with <u>venom</u>.

Tarantula hawks have one of the most painful stings of any insect.

TERRIFIC TEAMWORK

Have you ever seen a trail of ants? Ants use smells to follow the leader and work together.

HELPFUL INSECTS

Insects have a big impact on the planet.

PERFECT POLLINATORS

Many insects spend their time moving between plants. When they visit a plant, they get covered in pollen. They take that plant's pollen to the next plant. This helps more plants grow.

BIRD FOOD

Insects are one of the main food sources for birds. Without insects, birds would starve.

PROTECTING PLANTS

Many insects, such as ground beetles, help keep <u>crops</u> healthy by eating <u>weeds</u>. They also eat smaller insects that could harm the crops.

LIFE CYCLE OF A BUTTERFLY

There are many stages of change that happen throughout a life. One stage is having young. These phases make up a life cycle. A butterfly's life cycle is called complete metamorphosis.

LARVA
When the eggs <u>hatch</u>, tiny larvae come out. A butterfly larva is called a caterpillar.

EGG
Butterflies start as eggs.

16

PUPA

The caterpillar grows into a pupa. Then it makes a case around itself called a cocoon. Inside the cocoon, its body changes.

Then the cocoon splits open. A butterfly comes out.

ADULT
The adult butterfly lays its own eggs.

LIFE CYCLE OF A GRASSHOPPER

Some insects have a different type of life cycle. A grasshopper's life cycle is called incomplete metamorphosis.

EGG
Grasshoppers start their lives as eggs. Pods can hold 10 to 300 eggs.

NYMPH
After about ten months, the eggs hatch. The young insects that come out are called nymphs.

Nymphs grow out of their skin several times as they get bigger.

ADULT
Then nymphs start to grow wings and become adults. Adult grasshoppers have their own young. The life cycle continues.

BELIEVE IT OR NOT!

Julia butterflies live in the Amazon rainforest. These butterflies drink turtle tears to help their bodies get enough salt.

Dung beetles are some beastly bugs! These animals live in, lay their eggs in, and even eat poop.

Scientists have only discovered one type of insect that spends all year living in Antarctica. This insect is called the Antarctic midge.

Fruit flies were the first living things sent into space.

ARE YOU A GENIUS KID?

You now know lots of interesting insect facts that you can use to impress your friends and family. But first, let's test your knowledge. Are you ready to find out whether you are a genius kid?

Check back through the book if you are not sure.

1. How many legs do all insects have?
2. What are the two different types of insect life cycles called?
3. Name one way insects help the planet.

Answers: 1. Six, 2. Complete metamorphosis and incomplete metamorphosis, 3. Pollinating plants, being food for birds, eating weeds and harmful insects

GLOSSARY

adaptations   changes to animals that have happened over time to help them be better suited to their environment

camouflage   to blend into the surroundings to hide

communicate   to pass information between two or more living things

crops   plants that are grown by humans to be eaten or used

hatch   when a baby animal comes out of its egg

mandibles   the jaws of some animals

mouthparts   the parts near an animal's mouth that are used for feeding

tropical   very warm and wet

venom   a harmful substance that is injected through a bite or sting

weeds   plants that grow in an area where humans have not planted them

INDEX

abdomens 7
colonies 8
dances 9
eggs 12, 16–20
food 10, 15

heads 5–6
legs 5, 7, 23
plants 10, 14–15
space 21
thoraxes 7

water 10
wings 5, 7, 9, 19